Designed by Flowerpot Press in Franklin, TN.
www.FlowerpotPress.com
Designer: Jonas Fearon Bell
Editor: Katrine Crow
ROR-0808-0107
ISBN: 978-1-4867-1261-8
Made in China/Fabriqué en Chine

Copyright © 2017 Flowerpot Press,
a Division of Kamalu LLC, Franklin, TN, U.S.A. and Flowerpot
Children's Press, Inc., Oakville, ON, Canada. All rights reserved.
No part of this publication may be reproduced, stored in a retrieval
system or transmitted, in any form or by any means, electronic,
mechanical, photocopying, recording, optical scan, or otherwise,
without the prior written permission of the copyright holder.

Someone that I meet when I am walking down the street is a
BUS DRIVER.

(They drive me to school.)

Someone that I meet when I am walking down the street is a TAXI DRIVER.

(They drive me different places.)

Someone that I meet when I am walking down the street is a FIREFIGHTER.

(They help me in emergencies.)

Someone that I meet when I am walking down the street is a FARMER.

(They grow food for me.)

Someone that I meet when I am walking down the street is a
POLICE OFFICER.

(They keep me safe.)

Someone that I meet when I am walking down the street is a SOLDIER.

(They protect me.)

Someone that I meet when I am walking down the street is a FLORIST.

(They sell me flowers.)

Someone that I meet when I am walking down the street is a TEACHER.

(They help me learn.)

Someone that I meet when I am walking down the street is a DOCTOR.

(They help me to be healthy.)

Someone that I meet when I am walking down the street is a CHEF.

(They make food for me.)